THE *Powerful* LESSONS I'VE LEARNED

ONLINE DATING AFTER DIVORCE

MICCA VANVIELD

Printed in Canada

First Printing, 2017

ISBN 978-0-9936986-5-1

To Anita,
It was such a pleasure meeting you and for sharing this evening with you.
Keep Shining your light
Nicola

Dedication

This book is dedicated to my aunt,
Marcia Maureen Haughton.
Thank you for teaching me how to look to God for strength
and for showing that strength through your
battle with cancer to the very end of your natural life.
You are loved forever.

Prelude

#SMDH

So, yes, you read the title correctly. I am a divorcee who had her first actual dating experience at 32 years old. And, yes, this was all after being married for six years (in an eleven-year relationship). OH YES, that relationship!

Now, don't get me wrong; I've been on dates but with the person that I considered my significant other. But, to be honest, this decision of monogamy was decided straight from the beginning of our relationship. At the time, we believed in only being with each other, and we definitely didn't believe in breaking up or divorce. WELL, at least that's what I thought...

In order for you to truly understand this book, I will have to take you back -- way back to how it all began. See, this book is definitely not meant to bash the online dating process or to negatively critique the opposite sex. My hope for this book is to shed some light on some of what is out there in the online dating world and to help you understand what could be impacting your encounters. I am sharing my experiences to help you realize that there may be more to dating, especially online, than "just swiping right." (For my rookies or for those that have never experienced online dating, swiping right is the action you take when you are physically attracted to or drawn to someone's picture. If your initial reaction is "I don't think so," then the opposite is required -- you would simply swipe left).

By reading this book, you may start to relate to my experiences, become self-analytical and begin to think more critically. If you have had similar experiences, you will start to understand the emotions you felt at the time. You will laugh, you will get real and you will laugh and laugh some more. It is a beautiful journey, indeed, once you realize exactly what's out there. You will start to realize, just like me, that these experiences were brought upon you to help to shape you and your desires. You will realize that favorable experiences will help you to understand what you are looking for and may even get you right back on track in the "love" department. You will also realize that *unfavorable* experiences will help you to understand exactly what you *don't* want and that you have the power to choose the circumstances that are not aligned with what you want in the "love" department. See, many of us, that are currently dating have mixed expectations if any at all. Some of us are simply looking for a sexual relationship (you know, the hook up). Others are looking to date platonically (something deep, more meaningful) while others are looking for everything in between (as if anyone knows what that is). My hope for this book is that you know that you have the power to choose your mate and to create the relationship that you desire because you have discovered what's really out there and what is really destined for you. I hope that you can uncover the POWERFUL lessons in each of your dating encounters whether online or off.

Chapter 1

HOW IT ALL GOT STARTED

I am Micca Vanvield, a mother of three beautiful boys (my kings in training), and also, I am, what I like to call, a "serial helper." YES, I help absolutely everyone in any way that I possibly can (even to the point of not having enough because I feel someone else will be better served with my gift), but you may never assume this by looking at me. I am also known as that chick with the resting BITCH FACE. LOL! You know, when someone is constantly deep in thought due to their observant nature. It becomes so apparent on my face that people ask me, "what's the matter or are you ok?" Then, and only then, do I realize, "OH snap, I have to put that smile on. AGAIN."

See, I was born and raised in Montego Bay, Jamaica. Birthed as Chamica Champagnie but later transformed into Micca Vanvield. You will learn more about this later. For now, just think of Beyonce Knowles and Sasha Fierce. At the tender age of 11, I migrated to Toronto, Canada where I lived with my mom and her husband at the time. Growing up in Jamaica, I had no idea what "dating" was. I was raised by my grandparents who have been married much longer than I have been alive. My aunts and uncles always had boyfriends and girlfriends or someone just showed up with a baby one day and all of a sudden they were now a couple. So, as you can see the things that influenced me as a child and shaped my beliefs around relationships had nothing to do with dating. People are either together, or they're just not.

Like many others, I thought that I would just know how to love my partner and what I would want in a relationship. I thought that it would just come naturally, just like how I grew up. You meet someone, you like them, you get along and you simply fall in love. Oh boy, was I mistaken.

My impressions of love and relationships were based on how I grew up but also, largely, what I saw on TV. I was convinced that to be in love you had to constantly be kissing each other, always holding hands and touching each other. I have grown to realize that that is not necessarily the case in the real world.

I believe, that as children, we are programmed and shaped by our surroundings even while still in the womb. We are receiving both the positive and negative vibrations of our surroundings, and this, unfortunately, impacts certain decisions that are made later in life. Now, please understand that this can be backed by intensive research, but remember this book isn't meant to bore you with facts that may have no meaning to you. It's meant to help you realize that, like me, you gained a PHD (Probably Headed for Divorce) even before you knew what a relationship was. (I hope you laughed; that was so meant to be an LOL moment).

So how did I end up dating at 32 years old? Hmm. Fasten your seatbelts because I'm going to take you on my journey. Well the short version anyway. I really want to get to the juicy stuff. I was married for six years to the man I thought would be my life partner, you know, the love of my life. I started a relationship with my now ex-husband in 2004 at a time in my life when I had had a few failed relationships. I had already had my first son and really felt like I wanted to give up on life. I tried escaping it all with an attempt to move to England. I wanted to live with the "fun side of the family." However, the English Consulate had other plans. They did not accept my application for a work visa, so I was forced to stay in Canada. Some would say I was denied entry, but I would say that God had other plans. I was left with no choice but to figure out how I was going to make it in Toronto with a young child and literally no dream. Having a serious relationship was nowhere on the radar at the time because I was fighting the internal dialogue that I had let consume me, "No one will ever want to be with you because you have a kid." (It's crazy the words that we allow to resonate within us and play over and over. It's even crazier that we repeat them out loud.)

Dec 2004: So, I decided to go back to work after a three-week hiatus caused by what I thought was chronic back pain. As I reflect on the situation, I now realize that I was really sick and tired of life as I knew it and was craving a change. I wanted to move because I just wanted to start over, and I wanted to give my son the life he deserved, away from all the drama -- my drama.

When I was pregnant with my son, I had to give up on my dream of becoming a hairstylist on a cruise ship. I was not in a relationship with his father as I realized that he had another girl pregnant at the same time as me (Oh brother, I think I just realized that things were getting crazy even then). Before we split, I wanted to move away because the situation, to me, was bad. We were always arguing, he didn't feel comfortable around my family, and they definitely didn't like his attitude. I just wanted to get away from it all. I was looking for bliss, peace and serenity. Little did I know that I would get that right here in Toronto. All I had to do was go back to work and think about other things.

The day I returned to work was the day that changed the rest of my life. I wish I wrote journals because I would be able to tell you the exact date and even the time, but all I can remember is what I was wearing, how he looked and how I felt when he looked at me and just wouldn't look away.

We actually met at work when I was about six months pregnant with my son. We started out on the same team in a sales environment, but due to his constant stellar performance and me taking a break from work to take time off and have my child, he was always one step ahead of me. I had always thought he was a good-looking guy, but I never had the slightest thought that he would be interested in me (very low self-esteem. I told you I was taking you back. In those days, my self confidence was extremely low. In fact, it is for that woman who I was years ago, that I write this book!) I really wasn't thinking too much about him because I was thinking about how much I wanted to ignore what felt like aliens moving inside me, because of the pregnancy, and how much I, all of a sudden, was disgusted by fried chicken! (If you knew me, you would know why not being able to eat fried chicken was a serious problem!)

Flash forward to our reunion...

What I was wearing: Blue sweater, light blue jeans and light blue Timberlands. I guess I was in a blue mood that day. I would normally get all dolled up but, that morning I just didn't care. I didn't really want to go back to work. The thought of staying home and drowning in my sorrows was so much more appealing, but the universe has a way of making you do things that your conscious mind does not agree with.

What he was wearing: Dress shirt with vertical stripes, blue jeans and dress shoes. I even remember the muscles of his chest trying to escape the confines of his button down shirt.

He was visiting our office for our Christmas party/lunch, and we had a normal conversation. We chatted about random thoughts, and then it was time for lunch. There was salad, pasta and chicken. It was a 'go-around-the-table-filled-with-food-and-get-served' kind of a meal, so I got my food and sat next to my girlfriend. We started to engage in conversation, and then I looked up from my plate; my eyes met his. And then it happened: The heart flutter! He didn't look away, and I couldn't look away. I whispered beneath my breath to my girlfriend, "girl, why won't he stop staring at me?" I believe that that was the moment he took my heart. That's when it all started.

Now, you must be wondering, is this book about dating after divorce or a love story? I believe that in order for two people get to that point of separation or "divorce" in any relationship, there had to have been something that magnetized them together in the first place. That deserves to be celebrated, or at least acknowledged, in a positive way. But, let's fast-forward a bit so that this doesn't turn into the love story chronicles. Here is the quick version of where we ended up: We communicated for about three weeks. He came over and never left. We had our first child together -- his first and my second. We bought a house, got married, had a third child together and then IT happened. THE DIVORCE!

Chapter 2

FIRST DATING EXPERIENCE AT 32 YEARS OLD

You may be wondering where the rest of the story went, well, we will have to leave that for another book. Trust me -- it'll definitely be juicy. After an almost flawless relationship, at least I thought so anyway, the 'ex' had other plans. Maybe he felt like he was missing out on the joys of life as he jumped into being a father and a family man. Or, maybe he didn't realize that he was actually placed on a pedestal. Throughout our relationship, I suppressed myself to make sure he was always happy because if he was happy, I was happy. I would avoid saying or doing a lot of things just because I wanted to have a peaceful relationship not realizing that I was losing myself in the process.

After some time, I started to change. I didn't realize that I was transforming and becoming more of myself. This process was diminishing the kingdom that I had created for him, and I was, ultimately, losing him. In the beginning of our relationship, I was so focused on becoming "his wife." Funny, I was never that little girl that dreamed about getting married; however, when he came around, that all changed. I wanted to create a beautiful and loving home for him and our children. I wanted us to laugh together, travel together, and watch our children grow up together. I wanted us to grow old together, and the only way I knew that we could do that was to be his wife, completely. We both decided from day one that we would never be with anyone else but each other. We planned on getting married and staying married. Neither of us believed in divorce. During the course of our relationship, we started growing in separate directions. I started to dream of becoming an entrepreneur, and he was becoming comfortable with his current lifestyle and couldn't envision change. He wanted to be comfortable and secure. Not that there was anything wrong with that, but I was a dreamer, a visionary and he was not. All this led to the next stage of our marriage. I don't even think we realized what was happening. Seven years together and then.... He wanted a change, and while I was seven months pregnant and battling severe depression, he dropped the bomb. He wanted a divorce. Now some would say he was the worst guy on the face of the earth. Others would say he's an a@*hole (you know, not the nicest guy). I simply say he was confused and maybe even hurt. I decided that after about four months of trying to hold on to the marriage, that the love story, as I knew it, would be no more. Well, at least for the time being anyway. So I left!

Let's shift gears and fast forward.

Three years had gone by after I originally left. No, I was not single for those three years, even though at times, it felt that way. We were separated for two months and I hadn't dated anyone else. I didn't want the separation. I wanted my husband, but I felt that a break was needed at the time. I was still head over heals in love with him, the father of my children and the man that I had just spent the last seven years of my life with. This was definitely the longest relationship I had ever had. I was finding it difficult to move on even though I was approached with offers to date on a number of occasions. But, I didn't want them. I simply wanted my marriage back, and I prayed that my husband would come to his senses.

My wish came true. Two months later, he came crawling back. He wanted 'us' to work. Thank goodness. I couldn't have been any happier. I tried to do the whole, "I'm-so-mad-at-you-for-hurting-me-so-I'm-going-to-give you-a-piece-of-my-mind" act, but I just couldn't. I was just so happy and, of course, I took him back, I expressed very clearly my expectations of how I wanted things to be and he was on board, no more neglecting and being a "bad husband."

Things were going to change for the better. It started out great! We both felt like we wanted to be together again and make it work simply because neither of us believed in divorce (well, at least I didn't).

We had just got back from a vacation together in January which was great, but all of a sudden, he wanted to take a "solo" vacation in April. Hmm, the eyebrows raised and the gut started wrenching. We decided to take some time apart to figure out what we both wanted. I took a work-ation to St. Lucia, and he took his "solo trip" back to Jamaica. We both returned to Toronto on the same day. I had to start training for a new job the next day, so I headed straight out of town from the airport and returned home a few days later. Then he disappeared.

ME: home all weekend, only saw my husband for maybe half an hour. I was actually looking forward to chatting about our situation. Maybe bicker a bit and then have some great makeup sex. (Y'all know that's the best part of an argument)

HIM: Gone all weekend. Like literally ALL WEEKEND. SERIOUSLY?????

Question: Where the HELL are you sleeping?

ME: How the hell can we be experiencing marital problems and then you just disappear? I had a million and one questions racing through my mind. Where the hell are you? Who the hell are you with? And, why the hell aren't you at home trying to save your marriage?

The questions were all unanswered, but I was way too stubborn at the time to confront him because I felt so disrespected. I was now in victim mode. As per the discussions that we used to have, divorce was never an option for us, but, I guess with growing in different directions comes a change of beliefs. It was now Monday, and I returned to my training. Still no sign of my husband. He was MIA. I couldn't believe it.

This is when the switch up occured. The patterns had returned; I ignored them. The staying out late, going out every night, the playing "dominoes" with the boys, the "solo" vacations (or at least that's what I was told). I realized at that point that we may not be able to avoid the inevitable. I tried so hard to start fixing it; I suggested counselling, our pastor, even just having a conversation. He wanted none of it. He just decided to shut me out. He had made up his mind. HE WAS DONE.

One day, I got a call from his best friend (who never calls me), saying, "I'm just calling to check up on you because I hear that you are getting divorce." WHAT?! My mouth dropped… and that's… where… it… ended…

Eleven years, a marriage and three children and a house! Just like that; it was DONE. Now, don't get me wrong, I had come to terms that the relationship was not in a great place and that we needed help. But, that didn't matter now...and the pain began to creep in.

About a month and a half had gone by, it was summer of 2015, and I was devastated. My life had entered a whirlwind. My marriage had ended, my husband had moved on, and I was forced to deal with it. I was in pain. I was hurting all day, every day. I was filled with hate. I had loved him for 11 years. We had a life together, a family, and he decided to throw it all away without us even having a proper conversation about it?! He, all of a sudden, couldn't communicate with me anymore. I felt the depression coming back. I hated him, and I wanted him to hurt too. But, God had other plans. I did not foresee how this journey would bless me. The place that I was at in my life didn't allow me to see that there had to be an end to this storm. I felt that life, as I knew it, was over. I didn't want to learn the lessons. I just wanted the horrible feelings to end.

God places miracles in our lives in the form of devastation when He wants us to grow. When He wants to force change in our lives, our "norm" starts to shift, and we begin to feel pain. I take this as God's way of showing His love for us. He removes us from what we think is perfect, but was only perfect for a time, a season, and it develops us for the greatness that is to come! I now think about the pain, and it doesn't hurt anymore. I try to hate my ex-husband at times, and I just can't. No matter how deep I try to dig, I just can't find it in me. I finally accepted his decision. He had moved on, and it was time for me to do the same.

Chapter 3

MY EXPERIENCE WITH DATING SITE #1

MR. YELLOW

There is always a first time for everything. I was at a point in my life when I started to experience a lot of firsts. I realized that I was entering a period of growth. God wanted to do something new with my life by having me go through all of these experiences, so I had no choice but to welcome them all.

July 4, 2015: I caved. I did something I never thought I would do. I joined the online dating world. A girlfriend and I were hanging out on a Friday night -- just catching up. She wanted to know why my marriage ended, and so we did as girls do after a breakup, we started bashing men. YES, we cut them to pieces. Eventually, we decided that we would lighten things up a bit and wanted to have a little fun. So, she started to share with me her online dating experiences.

We laughed at all of her crazy encounters and messages, and she convinced me to set up a profile. Remember, I am very traditional; I've always had boyfriends, but I've never casually dated. I've also always met guys in the **#realworld**, and I definitely knew nothing about "the online dating experience." So, this was really new to me. When I thought about dating, I would automatically think of cheating (going back to the subconscious impressions of my childhood), simply because someone is going out with more than one person at a time. I had no idea what this new world entailed, and, oh boy, was I in for a rude awakening.

After having so much fun with her reviewing online profiles and awkward messages, I decided to try it out. Not for anything to really come from it, but for a distraction and a few laughs. I had recently found out that my now 'ex' was hanging out with my children and his new girlfriend. It hit me like a ton of bricks. I was furious. Yep, less than two months later, which meant it was serious. But, that's a whole other story. (Don't act like y'all have never been there ~ the outraged baby mother **#justkeepingitreal.)** I was definitely shocked and devastated, but I realized neither of those emotions would serve me. Up until that point, I thought he was going through another phase. It was at this point that I realized that there was no chance for reconciliation. It was definitely time for the distraction!

My first message was from Alice, and I thought, "what the hell did I do?" Maybe I didn't sign up correctly because now I have a girl messaging me. One's sexual orientation is a personal choice (to each their own), but I honestly thought that I made a mistake. I am attracted to males, so I thought that it was off to a hilarious start. Sure enough, I was wrong; it was an auto-generated message welcoming me to the site. I thought, "oh brother, this is going to be interesting."

Now on to the good stuff!

I felt like I was a piece of meat thrown into a pack of wolves. This was literally like a new world. The floodgates had been opened and waves of men came rushing in. The pics I posted were pretty decent. Nothing more than what I would have on my social media profiles. I actually took the time to fill out my profile and answered some of the questions; I thought that they would be beneficial to me finding a match. I guess when you're a rookie you literally think that this is like meeting someone in the #realworld. I didn't actually realize that there are serial profile stalkers and serial daters that exist in this new world. Messages from older men, younger men, and different races started pouring in right away.

WHAT?! ME?! I am attractive to these different types of men? Negativity and doubt started creeping in; I actually didn't realize the damage that was done to my self-esteem after my break up. I really just wanted to numb the pain of my new situation and sweep it all under the rug.

I was getting so much attention dating online. It was everything that I was sure I needed before, and I was certain that this attention would help me to complete myself. Due to my lack of confidence, I would always find myself trying to fill the void. A lot of times, that false belief of completion would come from attention I got from men. So, instead of working on the growth and development of myself (so that I could actually address those issues of insecurity) I started to find validation in these messages. Low self-esteem was pretty deep seeded in me, so I was looking for closure in places that I thought would make me feel beautiful. This wasn't out of the ordinary for me. I was the type of person that never had a break from a relationship. This void was new to me.

The more messages I received, the more I wanted. I was hungry for them. After communicating with all of the "Hi, How are you?" messages, I received a message from someone I will call, **"Mr. Yellow".** The unfortunate thing about online dating is that there's no way to know certain things about a person unless you meet face to face. I wasn't even sure if I was ready for this, but I thought "WTH! I have nothing to lose."

So, Mr. Yellow seemed like a nice person. He was an older gentleman, he had children and was recently divorced, so I figured we could relate to each other. I guess he was also a bit old school because he actually asked to have dinner instead of constantly messaging online. Which was nice but then one day he randomly called me, just out of the blue, and I was taken aback. My initial thought was, "How rude! He didn't even ask for permission to call." But, then, my self-talk did have 21 questions... ***Was I really ready for this? Was I rushing? Was I trying to be in too much control of the situation? Was I simply trying to fill a void? Did I just not want to be without someone?*** Well, like everything else, I decided to just go with the flow.

He wanted to pick me up at my place, but I hesitated because I was so used to being driven by my now ex-husband that it felt strange. I was in transition of getting my new car, so I did need a ride...uggg...I wanted to embrace my new life, so I agreed. Cheers to me for starting over! This was definitely the beginning of me stepping out of my old situation.

As I entered the car, I felt uncomfortable, and then my self-talk began, again. **Is it because I'm not ready? But, I need to move on? How was the conversation going to go? What if someone I knew saw us together?** For some strange reason, I felt like I was cheating on my husband (soon to be 'ex'), but I had to get out of my head. So, I said "screw it, if I am going to get over this, I will have to give it a fair shot." I decided to let my guard down.

Why my date is called Mr. Yellow. He showed up wearing yellow shoes, a yellow hat, and a yellow shirt. I like a man that dresses well. A very peculiar part of my DNA consists of me remembering these things, especially shoes. So my level of discomfort elevated. I was now being seen in public with my first date, at 32 years old, wearing three completely different shades of yellow. ARRGGHHH, I thought I was going to lose it, but I had to calm down.

We ended up at Wild Wings and had, what I thought was great conversation, to the point where the mismatch in the yellows didn't bother me anymore. We talked about our kids, jobs, past relationships and even how they ended. Now, I like to think that I am a great listener. I listened to him share and then I started to share. After all, I am thinking that this is what you do when you are on a date right?

I talked about my kids, work and, of course, my recent break up. And, then he dropped the bomb. He told me that it sounds like I was the cause of my divorce because I wanted to pursue an entrepreneurial career instead of getting a regular job, focusing on raising my children and taking care of my husband.

#ohnohedidn't My mouth dropped. Mr. Yellow had no clue who I was, what I was about, and he was now starting to judge me? I was furious, I got defensive. **"HOW DARE HE?"** Oh brother, just like that, this first date was over. I had checked out. **HOW RUDE!** He tried to continue the conversation but realized that my demeanor had changed. I was no longer engaged. He proceeded to ask, "so, when are we getting together again?" and I responded with, "I'm really busy, and I may not have the time." And then, strike 2! He was not impressed with my lack of excitement for a second date, so he responded with, "Do you not find me interesting? Or, did you come out today for the free meal?" My mouth dropped to the table. It was now time to leave. I really didn't want my Sasha Fierce to come out in public. All I could do was ask God for strength at that moment.

The waitress came over to check on our table, and I asked for the bill. I was done. It was time to go. He took out a bundle of $100 bills. I was sitting there like, "Really? Are you trying to impress me with your roll of cash?" I was so over it. I decided to go to the washroom and got back to the table to see that the bill was paid. Phew! At least he didn't ask me to pay. But, wait. Everything was still on the table, but **hold on,** there was no tip! #SMDH. #KMDT. This man is cheap as hell. Mr. Yellow completely struck out in the first inning. GAME OVER. I thought to myself, **"IS THIS WHAT'S REALLY OUT THERE?!"**

The first POWERFUL lesson I learned was to definitely look before you leap and not to rush. Never try to prematurely change a situation simply because it is different. In order for us to get what is really meant for us, we have to break (trust me, it cannot be avoided). Think of a broken limb, when it gets broken, you have to go through a process of healing while being restricted in a cast. Our lives are the exact same way. Our new situation (life) is the cast, and we have to go through the process of healing before we can start to live that new life, the one that God designed for us.

MR. WONDERFUL

I hope you've realized that all of my experiences could not make it to this book. There are some significant ones that left a lasting impression or were just plain crazy, so to them I would like to say, **"CONGRATULATIONS! You made it to the book!"** Thank goodness I didn't throw in the towel after one bad experience. Now, here goes #2.

...

I was back in the game. I had ignored Mr. Yellow's phone calls and texts and was now ready to move on. The messages kept pouring in. I got a little bored with the "Hi's and Hello's" again. But then it happened. On July 21, 2015, I got this:

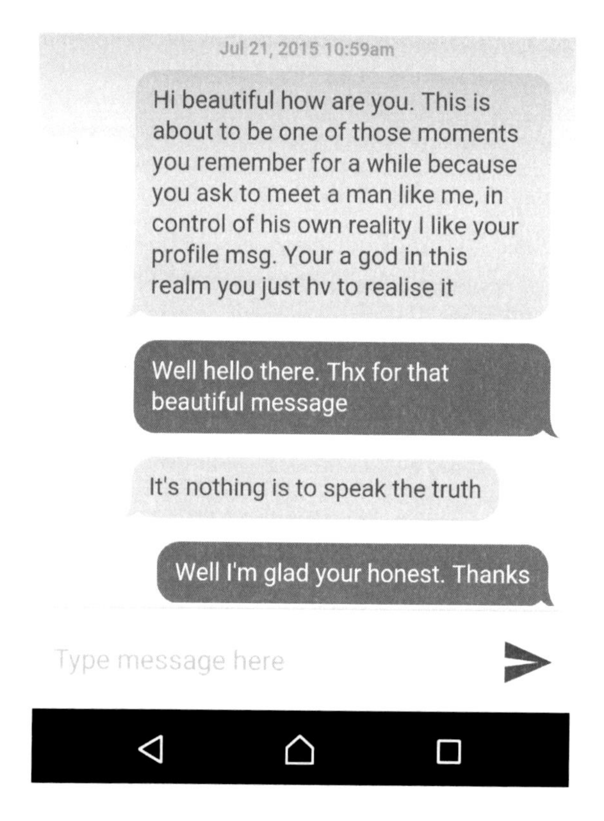

Right away I named him **"Mr. Wonderful."** I thought, "WOW." He was gorgeous and was elegant with his words. Sure his punctuation and grammar were non-existent, but I wasn't any better. This message was much better than the usual first impressions that I was used to and to top it all off, I had prayed just that morning and asked for the ability to forgive, to stop living in the past and for God to show me how to love again. WOW. All of this could not have been a coincidence...

So, I played right along. The interaction was great. We talked about The Secret, The Power, Neville Goddard, and how we had a lot of things to teach each other. OMG! He had now made it past the standard online messenger and had pierced my mind! As the conversation started to get heavy, we realized that we had quite a bit in common. We had children, were recently separated (or so he said) and loved speaking about ancient Egypt and Gods. We realized right away that there was a connection, and it was deep -- very deep. This was all outside of the fact that he was beautiful to look at. Well, his pics were, anyway. We messaged each other all day and figured why not meet in person and see where this thing could go.

Then it happened. It wasn't your traditional "date." I had an event that night, so I couldn't meet until after. He was living in an area that was on my way home, so I figured we would just find a place to meet.

His story was that he lived with his dad as a result of the separation. We decided to meet in the immediate area, and we would figure out what to do from there. I drove up, and he met me at my car. I was on the phone with my girlfriend telling her where I was and even sent her a screenshot of his pic. I thought I would cover my bases; my girl knew where I was and who I was with. I had sent her his name, where we were meeting and his picture. (Just in case I ended up on the news as being missing the next day). **Yes, I did that. Always take precaution, ladies.**

(Remember, I am new to this and also a bit paranoid. You may be cute as hell, but I don't know you like that. **#fareal**)

As I watched him walk over to my car, my first impression was DAMN. FINE. AS. HELL. He was casually dressed, and I was impressed. But wait! He was a little vertically challenged. "OK," I thought to myself, "calm down. You'll just have to wear flats when you go out. Besides, why am I already speaking US into existence?" I had to talk myself down. "Dear self, you're not marrying this person. You're simply going to have a conversation. No expectations. Right? RIGHT!"

And converse we did. We talked and talked and talked some more. We talked about life, experiences, business, family, dreams and aspirations. And I'm not going to hold out on you -- we also talked about SEX. Yep, I said it, the S word. Nothing happened that night, but it could have easily gone down. It was so refreshing to have a conversation with someone of the opposite sex and not argue, not cast blame, or even be judgmental. We connected on a soulful level, and if I didn't have to go use the little girl's room, (it was so late that everything was closed) we would have stayed and talked some more. We decided to call it a night, but we both realized that there was a deep connection. For sure.

My thoughts driving home were "WOW. He was really real, gorgeous, brilliant, business minded, driven and Sexy as Hell." All of this made him seem a little taller. The crazy thing is that he was only about an inch shorter than me, but at this point, that didn't really matter.

The next day I had to make the immediate morning phone call to my girlfriend with a full report mostly to let her know that I was alive. He was not a serial killer -- the complete opposite actually. He was sweet, and I couldn't get over how gorgeous he was. It was weird seeing someone else like that because I had viewed only one man in this way for last 11 years, but I was now playing the game with the hand that I was dealt.

He and I communicated all day. We expressed how thrilling it was for us to meet, and we shared with each other that we both felt that connection. YES! We talked about past sexual encounters and how long it had been and realized that we were both a little **#thirsty.** (Lol,**"#thirsty,"** the new age term for really wanting to get some.) Well, a lot thirsty. Being sexual beings in our marriages, it felt like a drought that needed a flood. We decided that if nothing else, we were going to do the damn deed. There was one small issue: we needed to find a place. No, we were not going to do it in my car, and no we were not going to do it outside. There was only one option left: a hotel room.

We met up and snuggled like two teenagers in love; I'm pretty sure that's what the clerk at the hotel thought, anyway. We got our room, had our bottle of wine, he got us some ice and turned some music on. We tried chilling for a bit-just talking but we realized that there was no need to fight it. It was finally here. It felt like a little piece of heaven. We were no longer going to be thirsty because that thirst was now being quenched. FINALLY, A RELEASE. Never did I think that I could feel comfortable, let alone, be with another man other than my ex-husband. I used to think that when I actually made love with another man I would feel like I was cheating because I was still in love, but I didn't feel like that. I felt amazing. It felt like what was missing all this time was finally here, and I didn't want it to go anywhere.

We went at it all night and all morning with very little sleep, requested a late check out for 3 pm., ordered some breakfast to the room around 1pm and then went at it again before actually leaving. OMG! I can't believe I did that. But I loved every minute of it. I felt liberated. This was, yet another, brand-new experience. **DID I REALLY JUST HAVE A ONE-NIGHT STAND? This was the beginning of me becoming a social butterfly.**

It was only supposed to be that one night; however, we communicated for a few months and realized that we may have something. I would always question the fact that I never went to his house, and he definitely wasn't coming to mine. I had a family member staying with me, and I had to be respectful. As great as he was, he was not on a bring-him-home-to meet-mama level. **ALWAYS TRUST YOUR GUT**. We took a few road trips together and spent our time in hotel rooms. It felt great, we were having fun, but I was beginning to feel unsure of where it would all go. One day, my suspicions of why I had never been to his house were heightened. I received a friend request from someone on social media and accepted. Right away, he came up as a suggestion because he was a mutual friend. I decided to go snoop around on his profile, and then I saw it. My suspicions were confirmed.

HE WAS MARRIED.

I was like, "**WTH? No way! How long was he lying? Was he ever separated? Am I now a homewrecker? OMG.**" I felt horrible. I was not about to do to someone else what was done to me. And, just like that. It was over. I made the decision to stay away! I was not going to knowingly be a side piece or simply there for sex. I was definitely not going to be the reason why a marriage ended and children got affected. When you know better, you do better and now that I knew better I was not going to give another woman the same hand that I was dealt. I realized that I was looking for a soulmate (not recognizing that it was too soon), and even though this seemed close, I was never going to find my soulmate in someone's spouse. I was out! **IS THIS WHAT'S REALLY OUT THERE?**

The second POWERFUL lesson I learned was that just because you pray and ask for something and you get what you think is what you asked for, that doesn't mean that the prayer was answered. Sometimes what shows up is actually meant to be a test. I recognized, after the fact, that this was my test, and I caved. I prayed for physical attributes. The one thing I now realized that I forgot to pray, for which is probably the most important to me now, is for him to be **GOD FEARING! A man of faith.** I was extremely impatient and living by the flesh. If you're wondering what living by the flesh means, it is when your attraction to a potential mate is heightened based on their physical appearance. **Mr. Wonderful** was easy on the eyes and great with words, so I chose not to look any deeper. I was really happy with the way the situation was presented on the surface, but as I learned, that type of satisfaction can only last so long. If you take the time to heal and realize God has a plan for you, you will start to recognize when things are not aligned with that plan.

MR. PRIMETIME

Now, at this point I was frustrated. I really thought there was something and then just like that, he lied. Another one, a liar, a cheater! Why can't people be truthful, say what's on their minds, and not hurt others? I was so over this. I removed all pictures from my online account and said screw it. I will meet someone the traditional way. Forget online dating!

...

Almost two months had passed, and I was beginning to wonder if I made the right decision. I was so focused on work and the success I was having, I almost forgot the fact that my social/romantic life was non-existent.

I was having lunch with a friend and, of course, we started talking about her dating life. I shared with her the story of my most recent break up, and right away she suggested I get back online. She shared with me her success stories, (or what she thought were successes at the time) and I shared with her what I thought was horror. She explained that I needed to be patient and just give it some time. She mentioned that she had met some really good guys online, and her current relationship, of about six months, was the result of dating online. I thought to myself, "why the hell not? Let's do this." I decided to give it another shot. I joined dating site #2.

September 2, 2015. The first message came in. "Hello Beautiful." I thought these men seemed a bit classier than the site before. There was definitely a mixture of older, younger and different races, but the biggest things I noticed right away were that A) I was getting messages from all over the world, and B) the minute I opened the app, my messages would be blowing up. WTH. Is there some sort of secret mechanism connected to the site and my device? Why is it that everytime I come on the site, these dudes know that I'm on? LIKE, seriously? This was slightly annoying. I browsed through the site for a few days, and then I received the weirdest message. The very first and only line in the message was:

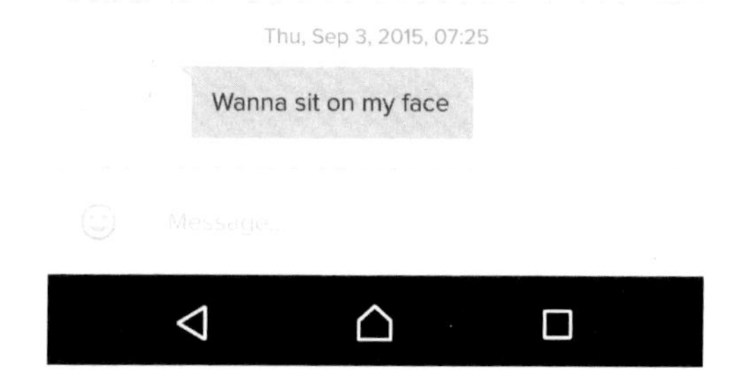

OMG. This is ridiculous. LIKE who does that? That's not how you introduce yourself to someone... Eeeewwwwhhh, right away? BLOCKED!

Sunday October 4, 11:12 AM. This next encounter had to be included because, boy oh boy, was it an experience. I had had a very long Saturday and was trying to recover by sleeping in that Sunday morning. I had appointments lined up that afternoon, so I figured, why not; I'm just going to take the morning off. When I looked at my phone after a well-enjoyed morning nap I noticed I had notifications. The very minute I opened up the app I felt like I was honey, and I had just entered a beehive. I took a look anyway because I was curious whom the message was from. I took a big gulp and swallowed. To my surprise, the first thing I noticed was this message:

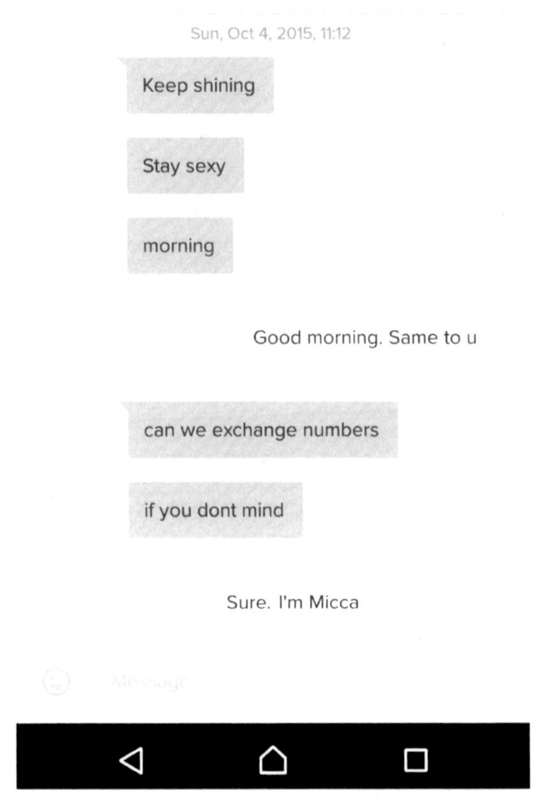

"Keep shining, Stay sexy, morning." "And who are you?!" I took a look at the picture. Now, I'm a little visually challenged (ok, I need glasses, but I refuse to wear them). I literally thought that my eyes were playing tricks on me because the pic I saw blew me away. He was beautiful. Light skinned (I figured he was of mixed race), totally inked and wearing a black tank (This was the TRIFECTA that made me melt as I was living in the flesh). WOW, OMG. He had a slender athletic body, thick, dark eyebrows, thick pouty lips and just this look of deliciousness on his face. I thought, "You messaged me? REALLY? THIS CAN'T BE REAL." I pondered the response and thought, nope, I won't respond. This has got to be a prank. You could never be interested in me. YOU'RE GORGEOUS, and I AM JUST NOT. (As you can see, the low self-esteem still had a large impact on my internal dialogue.) But, then I figured, "what the hell do I have to lose?" So, I responded.

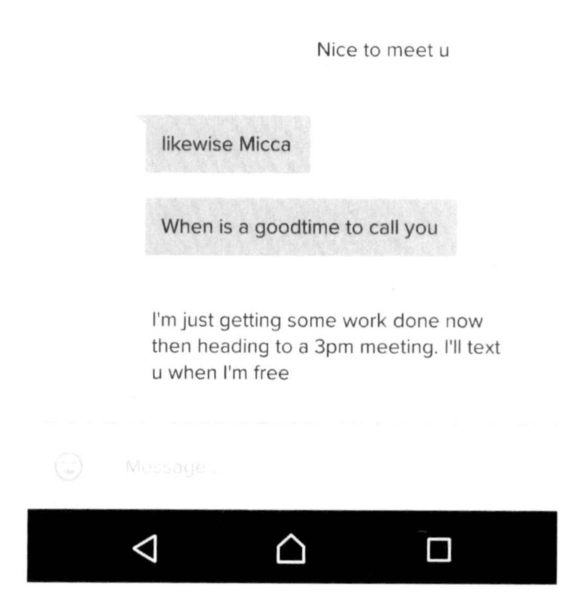

WHAT? He responded and asked for permission to call me **(Dear Fellas, ladies like when you ask permission. It shows that you are well mannered and respectful)**. Was he really real? We exchanged #'s, and I told him that I would text him when I was free.

I had just finished my appointment, and then my phone rang. I did not recognize the number, so I answered, "Micca, speaking." There was a response on the other line from a deep, raspy, yet sultry voice. "Hi Sweetie, it's ………" For the purposes of this book, his name is **Mr. Primetime**. At first, I was a little shocked that he called. But, now I was able to put a voice to those beautiful pics. We talked for a few minutes, and then I had to go. I was with a friend and didn't want to be rude. I told him that I was on my way to an appointment and that I would call him later.

I got home that night and started my routine to get ready for bed. Shower, head tie (YES, I said head tie, for women of African descent this is real) and wrapped up in my blanket. I messaged him, "I'm home now; we can chat if you're free." Within minutes, the phone rang. We sat on the phone and talked from about 11:45pm until about 4:00am. We talked about everything: life, family, upbringing, money, business, cars and, of course, we were so comfortable with each other that we took the conversation there. SEX. We discussed what we liked and disliked about lovemaking, and I uncovered that he was a freak. He had tried anything and everything with the exception of being with another man. He was a FREAK. We talked about all things sexual, fantasies and desires. I loved it. I was curious about where this would all lead.

We attempted to make plans to meet that week. He had family visiting from the states, so it made it a little difficult. His family was heading back home in about a week and a half, so we decided that this was the perfect time to get to know each other. We talked on the phone a few times every day, which made my desire to meet him grow stronger and stronger. He lived in the west end of the city, and I lived in the east, but distance isn't an issue that a working automobile cannot fix. And that was something we both had. The entire time we spoke on the phone I couldn't help but admire his pictures that were posted online. His features were to die for. He had the most delectable lips that you could ever imagine. I could literally feel them on my lips and the rest of my body. There was an intense connection. The energy was always felt through the phone in the midst of our conversations, and the tension was crazy. I wanted to meet him, and I wanted to meet him now. A week and a half seemed a little too long to wait for a meeting, so we both decided that he would pick me up after a night out with the boys, and we were just going to chill.

I was showered, groomed, overnight bag packed, and I was waiting with anticipation. OMG! I was finally going to meet him. That night I was so excited. I was overcome with the thought. I waited and waited and waited until I finally fell asleep. I think I may have even had a dream that he actually came to get me. I woke up around 5am and realized that I was still at home. I was MAD. "What the hell happened?" Our plans were tight. They were sealed, and I was ready to go! Why didn't I hear anything from him? No phone calls or messages! "Hhhhmmm, weird." I thought.

I went back to sleep. The next morning I woke up around 11am. Still no calls or messages. I decided to play like a big baby and sulk in my disappointment. I wasn't going to call either. The whole day went by, and I didn't cave. I decided that if he called or messaged, I wouldn't respond because I was pissed.

Sure enough, I received a message that evening which I didn't answer. YES. I was being strong. But, then he called, and my heart fluttered, so I picked up. "Hi baby," was the soothing sound on the other end of the line. "Hi," I responded. "I'm so sorry about last night. I was way too drunk to drive, so my friend took me to his house. I messaged you this afternoon when I woke up. I'm really sorry. I'm going to make it up to you." As much as I wanted to stay mad, I couldn't. I caved. My guard was down now. I felt like it was a really sincere apology and confirmation that he was ok. **This was the first sign I should have noticed, but ohhh naivety …**

The next day, we had a great conversation. "I'm really going to make it up to you," he said. "Let's take a drive down to Niagara Falls, tomorrow." Alright, he is really working hard to gain my trust back. I was like, "Sure. I have a meeting in the west end of the city tomorrow, so I will meet up with you afterwards."

It was going to be a great trip. We were going to go to the casino, dinner and whatever else came after. Maybe even stay the night depending on how things go. Tuesday came, and again, I got really excited. I was going to go on a client appointment, make some money and then meet up with my new crush. On the drive to the west end of the city, I was nervous, happy, anxious and apprehensive all at the same time. I got to the appointment—it went great. I closed business and thought to myself, "YES, I'm on a roll."

I had tried calling him on my way to my appointment just so he could keep me company on the long drive. I didn't get an answer, but I did receive a message saying that he was changing the tires on his car. I was like "Ok, Hun, do your thing, and I'll see you later." The appointment was wrapped up, and I was like, "OMG. This is it. I'm finally going to get to see him!"

I went to my car and called to find out where I would be meeting him. No answer. I called again. No answer. I messaged. No response. So, I called, again. No answer. SERIOUSLY?? WTH. How dare you not answer the phone? I was furious. I wasn't sure if I was more mad that he didn't respond or that I allowed myself to fall for his ish, AGAIN! That was strike 2. I WAS SO DONE WITH THIS. I sent him a message saying, "Do you not have a heart, or are you just a F@#!ING A*@ HOLE. I didn't receive a response. **I was hurt but officially done.** I couldn't believe it.

IS THIS WHAT'S REALLY OUT THERE?

The third POWERFUL lesson I learned was to always trust my gut. When you get that feeling in your stomach, almost to the point that you are feeling it in your bones, it's your intuition. **TRUST IT**. I've learned that God speaks to us through our intuitions. As His children, He has vowed to never leave us. He has stated that He will always take care of us. If He sees us going down a path that is not designed for us, He will make us feel uncomfortable. He has given us the right to choose what we think is right and what we think is wrong. The options are always right in front of us; it's all a matter of how we choose.

Chapter 6

CATFISH

About 2 weeks later, I received a message from **Mr. Prime-time.** "How's your day going beautiful?" My heart did flutter, but I was like, "HELL NAWH! You will not crawl back in that easily."

I ignored the message and went on with my day. We had communicated mostly through WhatsApp, so he would definitely see when I read his messages; I knew that not responding would drive him crazy. So, I didn't. The very next day, I received another message. "I am really sorry, about what happened. I was having a crazy day and issues with my car. I was so frustrated, so I came home and fell asleep. I was so embarrassed and saw that you were upset in your last message. I didn't know how to approach you. So, I stayed away. Again, I'm really sorry."

On one hand, I wanted to say BULLSHIT, but on the other hand, it was so easy for me to get over it because I was smitten. Sure enough, I responded. We talked for a while about how I didn't appreciate what he did and that all he had to do was communicate with me. Little did I know that this was a sign of what was to come…

The conversation took a turn, and we got back into planning mode because I was still so curious and wanted to see him. We decided that because our schedules were so crazy, we would wait a few days. In the meantime, we had real steamy conversations. We talked about how the lovemaking was going to be when we finally got together. YES, love-making. It felt like were both falling for each other, and it was headfirst. Well, at least for me, anyway.

I was chatting with a friend of mine, and we both decided that we needed a girl's night. We had both been so busy with our lives, so we needed a night out to unwind and catch up. We ended up at a nightclub where we danced and laughed all night. I told her about my new found experience and how infatuated I was. She saw my excitement and, as usual, she wanted to see a pic. I pulled out my phone and showed her the pictures that he had sent me. I wish I could show them to you, too, but I'm not trying to violate any one's privacy. Her reaction was amazing to see, "WOW. OMG. He's gorgeous," I responded with "I know, right? I'm still confused as to what he sees in me, but I guess I just have to go with the flow." (Oh, low self-esteem, you're bringing me down). The more we talked about the whole experience, and I shared stories with her, the more she got suspicious. I explained that each time we were supposed to meet, something always came up, and we never met. But, I still felt an amazing connection with this person. She started to laugh. When I say laugh, I mean hysterically. "What the hell is so funny? I didn't tell a joke." When she finally got to a point that she could compose herself, she said, **"GIRL, I THINK YOU'RE BEING CATFISHED!"**

CATFISHED???? What the hell is a Catfish?

She said, "It's not a Catfish; it's a show about people being Catfished."

What? A show! What kind of show?

She said, "I won't tell you. Go home, look it up online and watch an episode."

I had to go because my curiosity was killing me. **CATFISH! CATFISH! CATFISH!** What **the hell is Catfish?**

I walked through the door and rushed to get ready for bed. I needed to know what this was, immediately. I whipped out my tablet. Pulled my blanket over my legs and got comfortable. I found an episode online and started watching.

Sure enough, I fell asleep before the episode really explained anything -- I was exhausted.

When I woke up, it was morning, and the first thing I thought of when I opened my eyes was **CATFISH.** I started watching the episode again... It was good. Really good. This episode was about a guy meeting who he thought was a girl from an online website. They hit it off right away and communicated for about a year and a half as they were in different states. They had great conversations, shared pics with each other, and they were even falling in love. The person being catfished fell hard. He was always calling the **catfisher**, sending gifts, flowers and even decided that he wanted to meet her in person. He was excited. The **catfisher** agreed to a meeting in person. She was going to fly out to see the **catfishee**. She booked her flight and sent him a copy of the itinerary. The **catfishee** was on top of the world. In a few days, he would get to meet his love. He had dreamt of this for about a year and a half and now it is finally happening. The day finally arrived. The **catfishee** was excited. He went to the airport to pick her up. He had flowers in hand. The flight came in. The anticipation was exhilarating. He noticed that passengers started to come out from behind the screen. The more people that came out, the more anxious he got. He waited, and waited, and nothing. Someone came out, and he asked them for their flight #. It was the same flight that she was supposed to be on. "Where was she? I hope everything is ok," he said. His anticipation was now turning into worry. He waited some more but nothing. It had now been a few hours of waiting, and there were no more passengers from that flight that came out. He was worried. He tried calling her and no answer. He left messages, texts, emails and nothing. Now he was really worried. "WTH is going on? This does not make any damn sense." Finally, that night he received a message, "I'm so sorry, my love. I didn't make my flight. I was in a really bad car accident." Thank God. Now it all made sense. He asked if she was ok. She responded with, "Yes, now I'm fine. I'm just in a lot of pain." He told her that he wanted to fly out and see her. She expressed how grateful she was for him to be in her life and how that wasn't necessary. The

catfisher was adamant. She didn't want him to come to see her even though he was insisting. He was taken aback, perplexed. Why didn't she want him to come visit? He shared the experience with a friend, and the friend got suspicious and asked if he had a picture of her. The friend took the photo and did a reverse photo-lookup online. And, there it was, there were hits -- multiple hits. The friend clicked the link for these hits, and it landed on a social media profile. It was the **catfisher**, the same pic, but different name. The **catfishee** couldn't figure out what was going on and was furious. He needed to know more right away!

He called her; she picked up and heard that he was upset. "WTH IS GOING ON?" he asked. "WHO THE HELL ARE YOU?" and "WHY THE HELL HAVE YOU BEEN LYING TO ME?"

There was awkward silence. And then she admitted. "You're right. You're right. I've lied to you all this time. I'm not really who I say I am. I'm a man. A man who has always wanted to live the life of a girl. I posted pics online of the woman that I wanted to look like, and you bought it. I've been taking hormones so my voice has started to change. The airline ticket, car accident report and hospital report I sent you are fake, all photoshopped. I'm so sorry. Please forgive me."

He was devastated.

He had been Catfished.

Of course, I started to think. Could this be real? Sure enough, I did the same thing. I took all the photos and did a reverse photo-lookup just to satisfy my curiosity. And, voila, there it was. Just like that. There were hits.

I was CATFISHED. I couldn't believe it. The proof was right in front of me. He lied! "OMG. NO WAY." The pics all led to an app that I needed to download. Once I downloaded the app, I noticed that the exact same pics had someone else's name. **I COULDN'T BELIEVE IT.** I googled the name, and a link to a Facebook profile came up first. I had found the real person on social media, and now I was going to send him a message. YA, YA, I KNOW. I'M A SNITCH, BUT I DIDN'T CARE.

Hi You have no idea who I am. But I felt I should reach out to u. Just thought I'd let u know that I met someone on line a few months ago who claims to be from Toronto and he is using your pictures on his profile with another name. I basically used reverse psychology and reverse photo lookup on one of the pics he sent me and that's how I found out that it's you. I've realized that there are some sick people out there and unfortunately through this experience I've learned a valuable lesson. I hope he doesn't do u anymore damage or to any other female. Good luck in all your doing. Keep motivating. Take care

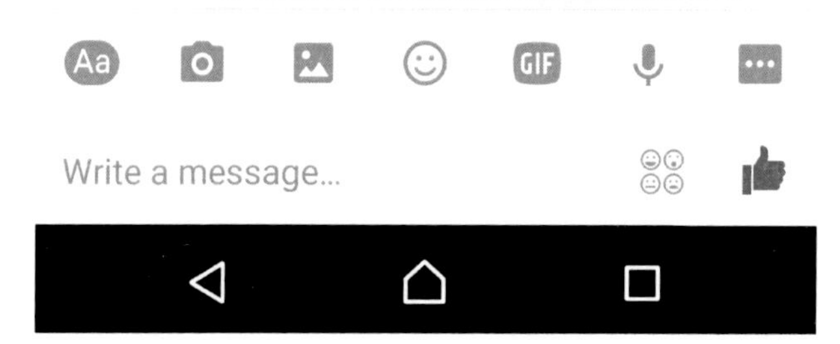

The great thing was, that unlike the episode that I watched, I hadn't spent any money on trying to go see him. I was just so upset that my low self-esteem and desperation for validation from men allowed me to get caught up. This unfortunate experience had to happen, and, of course it had to happen to me. But wait, just like with everything else in my life, it got worse.

I stopped all communication. He may have realized that I was upset about something, so I received the following messages from him:

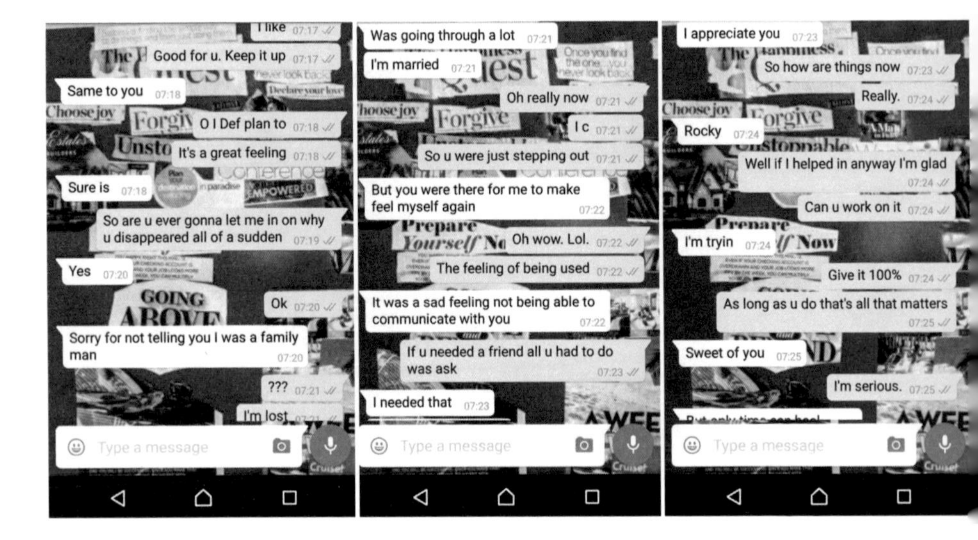

IS *THIS* WHAT'S REALLY OUT THERE?

The fourth, POWERFUL lesson I learned is that everything happens for a reason. Always trust the signs. This is why it is so important to focus on healing after a traumatic experience like a divorce, separation or loss. Your life and your mind experience a lot through this process and your judgement can be affected. I will be the first to admit that my judgement was definitely impeded. When you focus on healing after a divorce, one of the things that you can develop is a serious sense of discernment. You will start to receive confirmation on different elements that you are unsure about, and when you are faced with unclear situations, you will be more equipped to confidently make a decision that you know will be a good one for you.

MR. BATHROOM

As if I hadn't learned my lesson, I was now off to explore yet another site. I had heard quite a bit about this next site, so I decided to try it out. This is where I would say I had the most hilarious experience. This site had mixed reviews. However, there were a few success stories of people that were still together and even got married, so I figured why not give it a try?

The messages started pouring in. One by one, I read through them. Some of them had verbiage beyond the simple "Hi." I received a message from someone that read, "Hello, gorgeous, how are you?"

Damn…okay, he's gorgeous!

Here I was, again, living in the flesh. So, I responded. For the purposes of this book, let's call him, **Mr. Bathroom.** (Don't ask, you'll find out why later.) We communicated briefly online and then exchanged numbers so that we could graduate to messaging in the #realworld. It was great. He was really sweet, always checking in on me; calling me "sweetie," "babes," "hun." You know, the little words that could mean so much to most women. I wanted to avoid getting smitten again, but I thought it was cute.

After communicating for a few days, we started to plan an actual meeting. I was pretty busy and had to move some stuff around, but I made it happen. We had a discussion as to what our first meeting would be like, and we both agreed just to go with the flow. It was late in the day, and we decided that we would meet at his place. I made sure I was very clear before I agreed. I specifically told him that we could hang out, but there needs to be no funny business. He understood.

He gave me his address, and I headed over. I got there, and there was wine and an Android Box waiting for us to watch a movie. He listened. It was my favorite bottle of Moscato, and I must say, I was impressed. We sat and talked to the point where we couldn't even get through the movie. It was such a refreshing experience because he was really real. We had discussions about what we were both looking for, and it seemed that we were on the same page. We were both ready for a relationship. We agreed it was time to settle down…(Or so I thought.) We wanted to have a drama free relationship and wanted to work through our personal issues together. It was going to be great. At the end of multiple make out sessions, I decided that it was time for me to go home. I had an early morning meeting and needed to get a few hours of sleep. We had a few goodbye kisses and agreed to see each other on the weekend.

The weekend finally arrived. Meetings behind me (at least not until Sunday, so I could get to enjoy a little personal time). We had finished the bottle of Moscato on my previous visit, so I made a run to the liquor store before heading over. Of course, while I was on my way there, I did the routine check in with my girlfriend.

Address-check.

Pic-check.

He was also very good looking, but one of the first things I noticed about him was that he looked slightly different from his picture. He looked a little older in person. Not a bad thing at all -- he just looked more mature. I asked him about the picture. He mentioned that the picture was from a few years back, and he posted it because he doesn't really like taking pics. I thought, "Well, that's cool. I guess not everyone is a picture person." I bought the story and decided to leave it alone because I had absolutely no reason to not trust him. **Oh boy, was I wrong.**

I consider myself pretty observant, and I notice things that aren't necessarily visible to the naked eye. The first time I was over at his place, I was doing an internal scan to make sure that what I was told on the phone matches up to reality. When I entered the apartment I noticed the decor. It was very manly. No problem. This was a bachelor's pad… He mentioned he lived alone so that was adding up. It was a one bedroom apartment, and there were no traces of anyone else. Black and red leather furniture, black curtains that were way too short for the space they were in. They were supposed to be floor length, but he didn't care. No dining room table because he ate on his couch or ate out. No fabric shower curtain or mats in the bathroom. No towel to dry your hands and only one toothbrush. It all added up: he was a bachelor and his place confirmed it. I did, however, notice a crib in his bedroom and some toys in a toy box. He had already mentioned that he had a four-year-old son, but I asked whom they were for anyway. I was just testing him to see if his story would be consistent. He mentioned that they belonged to his son, and that he used them when he has him on the occasional weekend. I said, "a four year old in a crib?" He alluded to the fact that his son doesn't sleep in the crib anymore, but he was just too lazy to take the crib down. That was understandable because I had to take a crib down three times, and I despised it.

I was done snooping. It was now time to eat Chinese food, have some wine and talk and chill on the couch. Of course, we were both trying to fight the urge to give in to each other...then it happened.

We ended up in the bedroom. It felt right. It felt natural. We did the deed, and it was great! We cuddled, both fell asleep, and then I started dreaming. (I'm not trying to skip the juicy details, but what happens next is even juicier.) I had a dream that I was at his house, and I was lying down in his bed. There was banging at the door, and we ignored it. The banging went away, but then came back harder and harder.

In the dream, I thought, "WTH, who bangs on someone's door like that? Could it be the police? Is this guy a criminal?" (I've always somehow had a great fear of being with my guy and being caught up in a raid. I guess that's what happens when you have a liking for "bad boys.") But, he wasn't a bad boy. He had a job at a group home working with teen boys and not much of a social life.

"What's going on?" I thought. As I awoke, I realized that I was, in fact, asleep, and this must have been a dream. Phew, what a relief.

BUT WAIT, there is still a bang on the door. I got a little scared because now I was wide-awake.

I pushed him and slapped him to wake him up. He was a heavy sleeper, so it took a few minutes. The banging got louder and louder, and it wouldn't go away. I slapped him harder this time because I was getting scared. He started to wake up, and I told him that there was banging at the door. It took him a few seconds and then he jumped out the bed and said **"HOLY SHIT. GET UP, GET UP, AND GO IN THE BATHROOM."**

"WTH is wrong with you? What's going on?"

He ignored me and said, " Put on your clothes and go into the bathroom." At first I was like **HELL NAWH**. Yes, I will need to be dressed if this was the police or one of your boys. But, why go in the bathroom? I wasn't doing anything wrong, so why would I hide? There wasn't much time to think. I reluctantly went along with what I thought was a weird request. I grabbed by dress and my underwear. My bra was nowhere to be found. With my hands folded and my face mean muggin I slowly walked into the bathroom. I was standing around and was just about to use the toilet as a seat, and then he said "**NO. Stand in the tub**."

WTH! STAND IN THE TUB? OH HELL NAWH!!! I didn't have enough time to think. This was all happening so fast. I listened to him, like an idiot, and stood in the damn tub.

Oh was I pissed. All that was racing through my mind was how I was going to literally cuss the skin off this boy. I've always been a very feisty Jamaican girl, it can be really intense at times, so I try to suppress it as much as possible. But, it was going to come out today though. **HE WAS GOING TO SEE MY SASHA FIERCE**.

As I stood there for what was probably a few seconds, but it felt like days, I heard the door finally open. The banging stopped, and all I could do was listen. I heard a voice. It wasn't a man's voice and it definitely didn't sound like the police. It wasn't his son, either. As I tried to eavesdrop it came to me. **IT WAS A WOMAN**.

She asked him, " What were you doing? Why did you take so long to open the door? And, why are you sweating?" His response was **"I HAD TO RUN TO OPEN THE DOOR."**

Really?! He couldn't have come up with a better excuse? His bedroom door was literally ten feet away from the front door. I guess thinking on his feet and under pressure weren't really his strong suit. As I stood standing in the tub with some of my clothes on and my arms crossed, the fury literally pierced through my skin. I thought "what if I have to defend myself? What would I do?" I didn't even have time to come up with an answer. The voice got closer, but I couldn't understand what she was saying. She was speaking English but with a very thick accent. And then, I felt a presence.

She was in the bathroom!

She walked right to the shower and pulled the curtain back. And there I was. **FURIOUS** but in shock. I couldn't even utter a word. She looked a little more comfortable with the whole situation than I felt and then she said to me, **"ARE YOU HIS GIRLFRIEND?"** I said "**NO.**" with the worst attitude you could ever imagine. Arms still folded and ready to defend myself if need be. Her retort was **"WELL, I'M HIS WIFE."**

WTH! No way. This can't be. Without thinking about it, I stepped gracefully out of the tub. I guess she felt the fury and disgust in my energy, and she probably thought that I would get physical, so she said, "Oh no honey, I don't have a problem with you, I have a problem with him doing this, again."

AGAIN? This had happened before? OMG. I was so wrong. He wasn't a bachelor. He was a man with a child and a wife!

I came out of the bathroom and grabbed my belongings, my bra (I finally found the bra), my jewelry, my purse and stormed through the door. She stormed out right behind me. He came out the apartment after both of us saying, "I can explain!"

EXPLAIN? WHAT IS THERE TO EXPLAIN? You are a married man who cheated. Obviously more than once, and now you got caught. **AGAIN.** The only difference with this time is that I'm now caught up in it!

This dude had some nerve trying to hold onto my hand as he was trying to explain. **"I DON'T WANT TO HEAR IT. DON'T TOUCH ME. DON'T TALK TO ME. LOSE MY GODDAM NUMBER**." He was strong and holding on tight. I was finally able to free my wrist. I did not want to hear it or be seen anywhere near this commotion. It was embarrassing, even though it was 2am and no one was around. I stormed out the front door of the building, and she stormed out right behind me. As I walked to my car, I couldn't help but think about the half-drunk bottle of wine that I forgot to pick up. I thought "CHO" (as we island folks would say). Screw it. I'm so over this. I jumped in my car, and his wife proceeded to walk down the street alone. I drove north; she walked south, but wait, I noticed something. She had a duffel bag. **WHY WOULD YOU GO HOME (WHERE YOU LIVE WITH YOUR HUSBAND) AT 2am WITH A DUFFEL BAG?** Really? I was lost. But then again, I didn't care. The only thing I could think was:

IS THIS WHAT IS REALLY OUT THERE?

The fifth POWERFUL lesson I learned is that true healing does take time and dedication. When you are emotionally vulnerable, society tends to see you as prey. This time I swore I was doing all the right things; however, I was not right mentally and spiritually. I was looking for love. I wanted to move forward. I thought I was making progress after the divorce, and I was, but I didn't realize how much work, time and effort it would take. I was trying to control the situations in my romantic life by creating them on my own. I was not consulting God to ensure that they were right. When you are off course, our creator has a way of getting you right back on track.

MR. TEMPTATION

After all these experiences, and trust me, these were the only ones that made it to the book, I was officially over it. No more. I was on a different path; a journey to uncover spirituality on a much deeper level. I felt like I was at a crossroads in my life, and I wanted to go one way, but the universe wanted me to go another. Because of this new journey, I was introduced to a book called *The Purpose Driven Life* by Rick Warren. This book was introduced to me by two amazing ladies who had started a movement and wanted to build an army of warriors who were ready to share God's word with the rest of the world. We would read the book each day and then memorize the verses. The change was great and the journey started off on the right foot.

One day we got to a chapter that talked about growing through temptation. We were more than half way through the book, and I was making stride and loving it. I made a decision to be really committed and obedient because I'd realized that I wanted to make changes in certain areas of my life including my relationship with God but also my love life. I figured that I was going to leave all areas of my life up to God because He did say that **"I will never leave you nor abandon you," in Hebrews 13:5.** This journey had me deep into prayer. I was talking to God a number of times per day, and I loved it. On this particular day, I felt an urge to be in a relationship. I talked to God and restated the type of man that I was looking for in my life. I wanted him to be hardworking and ambitious yet fun loving. I wanted him to be caring and kind. He needed to love to travel and, of course, be God-fearing. This was #1 and a huge difference from my previous asks of men. I left it there.

I was going about my day as usual and realized that I had a notification from one of the dating sites. I hadn't been on for months, so I thought I'd check to see if this message was similar to what I had received from Alice. Remember, my welcome message?

When I opened the app, it wasn't Alice. It was someone who we'll call '**Mr. Temptation.'** Little did I know, he was going to be the temptation that I would need to overcome as I embarked on this next stage of my journey.

(But, he sure was beautiful. Sometimes I caught myself slipping back to living in the flesh, but Lord knows that I wanted to change.) He was light skinned, looked amazing in a suit and had dread locks. Hhhmm. I've never really communicated with a guy with dreadlocks before, so I was surprised how attractive I thought he was. I zoomed in on his pic and thought he had the most beautiful eyes. I was just taken. I figured, DAMN. At this point in my life, I had brought myself to a place where I was confident and my sense of independence was getting stronger. If this were a few months ago, I would be wondering, "Why is he messaging me? What does he see in me? He's too gorgeous to be communicating with me." Instead I thought, "we are on the same frequency. I attracted him to me. I asked for him." WELL, the joke would be on me. Not all that glitters is gold. Here goes the test.

I received the following message....

Jun 8 3:17pm

You too
beautiful to be on a dating site let
me end your search hun, i'm looking
for a FRIEND that would lead to
something serious you never can
tell i can be the answer to the end
of your search if you believe FATE
brought us together for a reason
take that BOLD STEP TODAY text
me Age and distance can't never
stop i'm willing to relocate for the
rightful one ,You can text me
anytime or you can email me u can
email me
Getting a text from you would really
make my day!!

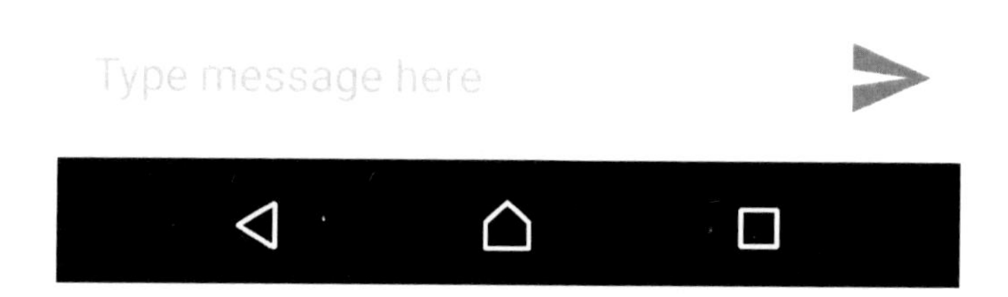

How refreshing? A man's man who has a way with words -- well another one. I responded to his message through the app, but then I thought, "Wait. He did say to email or text. Now that I'm on the journey of obedience that's exactly what I will do." So, I sent him an email. I didn't want to text even though he had his # in the message. I was still traumatized from my previous experiences, but I figured I'll give it a try, again. A few hours went by, and he responded to my email with the following:

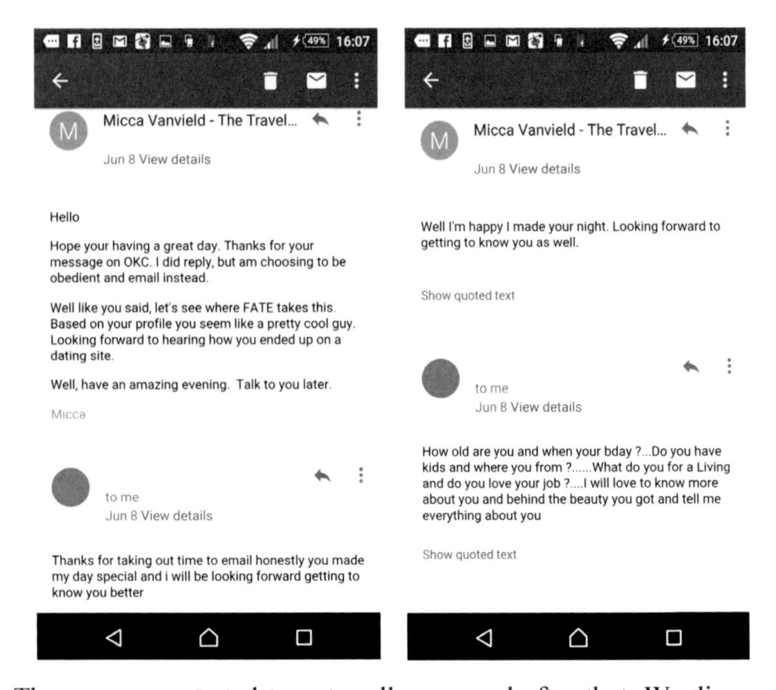

The messages started to get really personal after that. We discussed age, birth, upbringing, family, children, work, where we lived, everything. His birthday was coming up, and he would be 35yrs old. So, we were close in age. He was born in New York and raised in Kingston, Jamaica. He was a divorced father of a 5-year-old girl and was 5'11. My mind started planning ahead; at least I could still wear my heels if I were around him. (It's funny the things that us women think about straight from the get go.)

He had moved to Atlanta, Georgia for business and to get away from the bad memories of his ex-wife and the whole ordeal their divorce put him through. His daughter meant the WORLD TO HIM. Yes, he was a family man. He worked as a Computer Consultant for a Chinese company years ago, but his boss' wife was sexually harassing him, so he had to stop working there. Things got really bad for him when his ex wife left him and his daughter to get married to someone with more money. He loved to travel and had been to many countries in the world. He was presently doing a contract in Nigeria. He mentioned that he planned on returning to the US once he was done with his "project" in Nigeria.

Remember, when we pray God can send us a test that resembles the answer to our prayers. He does this so that we can learn the lessons that we need to in order to prepare us for our blessing. Could this really be everything that I asked for? Because of what I was learning along my new journey, I realized that it was possible. The more we talked, the more I realized he loved God. He even sang in the choir at his church in Atlanta. He sent me a video of him singing to prove it. I had no reason to doubt him. He seemed real and really convincing. I couldn't believe it. Was he the man that I knew was out there for me?

We had now elevated our conversation from emails to phone calls. One thing I noticed about his emails, though, was that his grammar was a little off. The emails were lengthy, and I couldn't understand them completely. I thought "not a huge deal;" nonetheless, I did notice it. (See the signs are always there for us to dig deeper, we just choose to ignore them.)

Our conversations were great. We talked about where he was in Nigeria and why he was there. He was into the automotive industry. He bought cars from overseas and had them shipped to Nigeria. He would then sell them in Nigeria and Europe for a profit. It sounded like a legitimate business and a great way for a man to make an honest living. I knew nothing about the industry, so all I could do was believe whatever he said.

I asked him about where his daughter was when he had to work, and he said daycare. He had her in daycare sometimes six days a week because he had no one to help take care of her. I wondered why he didn't leave her in the United States, but he mentioned that he had no family there. His mother and brother were both in Jamaica so that wasn't an option. I thought, "Cool, you can take her to Jamaica and leave her with your Mom." This is a common practice in the islands. Parents often leave their children with family to go and build a better life in another country. But, he said, "NO." Even though his mom was only in her late 50s, she wasn't all that well, and his brother was unreliable. He also told me that his dad died in a car accident in 2010, and the brother was driving. He blamed himself for his dad's death and had been depressed ever since. I tell you, this was such a sad story that I was falling for more and more each time we spoke.

We had talked about being in a serious relationship even though it would be long distance. As soon as he got back to Atlanta, he was going to fly me out to see him. I was excited. In a few weeks I was going to take a trip to go see this amazing man. The more I learned about him, the more I opened my heart. He was a single father in a strange country with a 5-year-old daughter and no other family around. He was doing it all for his business. His dream. I could do nothing but appreciate that about him because I could relate to the sacrifice. When we talked about our relationship, we talked about him relocating as I was not about to move from the city I was living in. He was totally on board, and I was more than ready to help him take care of his little girl. She would be like that daughter I've always wanted, but never conceived. I was willing to take on that challenge no matter what form it came in. Besides, I'd be helping him out and giving her a stable home while he worked. The more we talked about it, the more it sounded like a great idea.

Then, one day something felt strange. Reality was about to set in. I hadn't received an email, message or a phone call. Something was off. This wasn't like him. I thought about reaching out, but I knew he had a busy workday. I figured I would hear from him when he woke up the next day especially because of our time difference, which was about six hours. I got in from my event that night and settled in for bed. I was only asleep for a few hours and my phone rang. It was him, **Mr.Temptation**. "Hi baby. Are you sleeping?" "Yes, I was, but I can talk now. How are you? How was your day?"

"Well, that's what I'm calling you to talk about."

"Ok, what happened?"

He said that he went to go clear the shipment for his cars, and he had to make a payment to the government to avoid any hassles. He already had a set amount of what to pay. In previous conversations he had mentioned that people get greedy. They have no heart and could change previously agreed upon prices on a whim, and you have no option but to agree especially if you wanted to continue doing business. He had also mentioned in one of our previous conversations that his mom and brother were supposed to give him some money as he was running low. He had sold a few cars, and he was expecting the payment in a few days, so it would literally just be a short-term loan that he would be receiving from them. **(OH THE SIGNS THAT I CHOSE NOT TO SEE.)** They weren't being very cooperative, so he didn't know how he was going to get by. He had basically spent all his money on the deal with the vehicles, hotel, daycare for his daughter, a driver and what he would need to pay the government. He was running low on funds and needed some help.

Little did I know that he wasn't only communicating with me; he was setting me up!

The next day, we had another phone conversation. This time it was about him actually needing *my* help. He had gone to pay the officials, and, of course, they wanted more money. He wasn't able to come up with the money they were asking for, and his mom and brother turned him down. He slickly asked if I could loan him some money until he received the payment for the vehicle that he sold, and then he would pay me back. **My suspicions were confirmed.** The minute my stomach didn't feel good about the situation, I started to do some research. **TRUST YOUR INTUITION.**

I discovered that there was a scam called the **Romance Scam** that stemmed from Nigeria. According to my research, there are women that have sent tens of thousands of dollars to these scammers. The scammers (who normally post pictures of really good looking guys) will message you on these dating websites letting you know how beautiful and special you are, and they will ask you to contact them. They will give you their email address, phone number, contact name for other messaging apps, you basically have all the ways to get a hold of them. They will have some kind of story for you to feel sorry for them and then a family member will be really sick. They will even talk a lot about God. You will be totally smitten by them, and then, when they think that they have you whipped, they'll pull out the big guns; the "I LOVE YOU!!" Yep, they will tell you that they are in love with you and can't wait to spend the rest of their lives with you. If you choose to be naive, then you will believe them, if not you will notice that these are all signs of deceit. These men are extremely charming and will always be great with words. Once you respond to their message, they will communicate and feel you out to see when they can go in for the 'kill.' They will tell you they expected money from somewhere else, but it will fall through, and they will feel terrible asking you, but they will ask anyways. You will feel sorry for them and fork out the cash.

When he asked me for the money, I was on to him. I thought to myself, **"I don't care how good looking you are, you will not scam me, today."** Right away, my tone took a different turn, I said, "Listen honey, I'm a single mother of 3 who has to work her butt off to support her children financially. Therefore, I have no additional disposable income, even if it's short term, to give to anybody." I wasn't being mean, I was just being real. He said "OK. I'm going to let you get some sleep. We'll talk soon."

And, just like that. It was over. No more phone calls, emails, messages. He had confirmed my suspicions whether he knew it or not. He was one of them. A scammer! Thank goodness I listened to my intuition, and I didn't fall for it. It did, however, make me think. **He was my TEMPTATION**. He thought he had me, but God had other plans. I realized that my recent months of trials as well as my focus on self-love was starting to pay off. I was beginning to see the powerful lessons in these experiences. The bible says **"God is faithful. He will keep the temptation from becoming so strong that you cannot stand up against it. When you are tempted, he will show you a way that you will not give in to it." 1 Corinthians 10:13**. I didn't give in. I was strong. The devil was a liar, and I was now determined to use this experience to help other women.

But, I still thought to myself, "**IS THIS WHAT IS REALLY OUT THERE?"**

The sixth POWERFUL lesson I learned was to really be patient. Trust your gut and be really patient and faithful to the process of healing. Try to develop a newfound sense of independence before you even entertain the thought of another long-term relationship. After separation, you will be in a very fragile state whether you like to admit it or not. We, oftentimes, think that we are ready, and the majority of the times we are confused and have mixed feelings. We develop a fear of failure or start to feel that we are not good enough. We start to feel as if we are going to prove our haters wrong. Please don't rush into a relationship. Be patient.

Chapter 9

MY POWERFUL LESSONS

I realize now, that there were lessons in all of these experiences. As unpleasant as they were at the time, I now realize that I didn't just experience them for me; I experienced them so that I could share them with others in order for them to find inspiration and healing. I've always thought that I was a strong woman, and I've lived my life masking any sign of weakness or defeat. I want you to understand that it doesn't matter how strong you are, we all have a breaking point, and it is absolutely OK to feel like you're breaking. Your greatest lessons come from what you may think is defeat. That defeat is actually the preparation for your victory that is on its way. You just have to make a decision to trust the process.

My breaking point came in my fourth pregnancy. I was about 7 months pregnant with my third child. Like many women, I too experienced miscarriage and as devastating as that moment was, I realized that in all disappointments there are silver linings. During my fourth pregnancy, I was diagnosed with severe depression and had to start taking medication just to numb the pain that I constantly felt day-to-day. Without experiencing this ultimate low in my life along with the loss of my unborn child, I would have never realized that I needed to slow down and stop trying to do so much. I was mentally exhausted and was just too busy to realize it. I stopped thinking that I was invincible and that I could never experience loss. I started to appreciate my children, the current family that I had around me and stopped feeling the need to play super woman. I realized that I needed to take time and actually appreciate what and who I had instead of focusing so much on what I thought I wanted.

I now look at life experiences a little more analytically to find the message or lesson in each of them, whether it is positive or negative. I believe each one of my online dating experiences have taught me very valuable lessons and have also helped me to discover something new about myself. There is a process that you go through after divorce/separation/loss, and I wanted to bypass all the steps and just be OK. Unfortunately, we were not designed to work that way.

The first online dating experience came at a time when I thought I could sweep all of my troubles under the rug, and they would just go away. I thought that because I didn't want to deal with the pain of being deceived, lied to and betrayed. I was just going to ignore it. I withdrew. I wanted the pain to go away and the crying to stop. I wanted my gut to stop feeling full and my body to stop feeling so nervous. I figured I would just completely ignore that fact that I had just ended an eleven-year relationship. Even though **Mr. Yellow** stated that I was the cause of my divorce, and I was upset when he said it; the whole experience made me realize that I did play a part in the disruption of my marriage, and even though my ex made final the decision, it wasn't all on him. Throughout all our troubles, I was pointing the finger at everyone else and didn't look at myself. He was always too busy for me. He would always speak to me harshly. He didn't want to spend time with me.

I realize now that I played a part in the demise of the relationship by not taking responsibility for my own actions and my own neglect; for wanting to do a lot of things on my own and not working together with my husband as a team. I realized, with this first date, at 32, a part of why my marriage ended was so I could begin preparing for MR. RIGHT. Therefore, I needed to start paying attention, as I didn't want to take any of these flaws into any future relationships.

The second online dating experience taught me that I simply wasn't ready to jump into any new relationships. I moved onto to the next phase in the process, which is where you put yourself out there -- become social, hoping that this would numb the pain. I needed a distraction and that's what **Mr. Wonderful** was. He was just a beautiful being to look at, to talk to and to share the same space with. I loved his mind; the way he used his words. Initially, I thought, "I finally get to experience a **#onenightstand.**" (See, when I got married young, I thought that I would be missing out, but there was a lot more in store for my life than I could ever imagine.) Mr. Wonderful and I had a few dates. This was the first time in a very long time that someone actually made me feel like I mattered. I actually felt like someone cared. The attention, the early morning and late night messages...I could get used to this. My heart was being tested. Could I really be open and honest about my feelings for someone else again? I definitely didn't want to admit it, but he sure was a test for me. He was a test for me to see how far I would go with him and where I would allow my heart to go. Eventually, I passed that test. The signs were there, but it took a while to see them clearly. The minute I thought that he might still be married, I started to ask questions, and he confirmed it. At that point, he got dropped like a hot potato straight out the oven. Thank goodness for my intuition and for being at a place in my life that I started to trust it even more. When I wasn't in touch with my intuition, it took me a while to figure out what was going on. All I knew was that I needed to work on me.

My third online dating experience was definitely a new one for me. It was the eye opener to let me know that these types of individuals are really out there, but I was attracting them to me. There are individuals that have such a sick agenda, and they will prey on one's vulnerability. I still have yet to meet **Mr. Primetime** in person and had cut all communications. To be completely honest, I don't think I will ever meet him. In the beginning, when I had cut all communication, it was hard because I really felt as if I was falling for him. The fact that he had to lie and lead me on was very low. However, I again realized that my intuition needed to start kicking in sooner. The lesson I learned here was to stop getting so drawn to one's physical features that I completely miss the true nature of the situation. I also realized that I was now attracting a certain type of man or even a certain type of situation because I was so focused on the outcome.

I had started to learn about the law of attraction and about universal frequencies. The basic concept is that you will drive energy to your most dominant thoughts, and that is what will manifest in your life. I was driving energy to cheating and how I felt like I was cheated on and betrayed, so I was attracting cheating men. I was focused on being hurt and betrayed, so I was constantly attracting men that would betray me. I started to think that I needed to change my thoughts fast if I wanted to change my experiences from negative to positive.

Mr. Bathroom was the shock to the muscle I needed. The nail was hit right on the head, as my intuition was so strong I saw the situation in my dream right before it even happened. It was definitely the most embarrassing of the experiences, but that was exactly what I needed to realize the message. It was telling me to take the time and work on **ME**. I was looking for attention, validation and stabilization. I didn't realize that it was from the wrong sources. I knew that I needed to look to spiritual sources for guidance and direction rather than looking to outside sources. After that experience, I started to do just that. I started to explore a variety of sources so that I could have a better understanding of people and life in general. I took a self-development course that really helped me uncover some of the things in my life that may have led to my current situation and that was the relationship (or lack there of) that I had with my father and my grandfather. I realized that the men that I used to look up to were now being viewed as disappointments and failure in my eyes, and I needed to address that. If it wasn't addressed, I would constantly be ending up with disappointments and failures. It would be what my subconscious would attract. I realized that I wanted to have more spiritual guidance. Not too long after that experience with Mr. Bathroom, I started to meditate and pray a lot more. I prayed, everyday, for guidance, strength and for the ability to hear God's voice. He speaks to us through our intuition. That's how we get the direction that we are asking for. I used to think that I didn't really know how to pray, and I would even question if I was being heard. I learned that when we speak to God through prayer, He responds to us through our intuition, our gut feelings, through what can often be mistaken as our mind playing tricks on us. I didn't realize it, but at the time I believed that the yearning that I had for change was God trying to tell me to look to Him, to draw closer. I knew deep down that I deserved more, better -- the best actually. The only way that I was going to get that was to do it on God's time, not mine.

The experience with **Mr. Temptation** was definitely that. A temptation. It was a test to see how much I had grown spiritually and if I was actually strengthening my gut. I wanted to hear GOD in all situations. I wanted Him to speak to me, to show me when I was heading for danger. He did just that. Mr. Temptation was gorgeous. He had the most sincere looking face and a compelling life story. He was a single dad who was doing what he had to do take care of his family, and all he wanted was someone to love him. At least that's what he wanted me to think. The signs were visible, and I noticed them from the beginning. It was working, GOD was showing me the way, and I was grateful. I caught on early. The long winded emails and messages, the seductive pictures and even pictures of his daughter, his love for GOD and even singing on the church choir. MAN. I almost got fooled, again, but not this time. I had changed the focus of my thoughts. I was on a different frequency. I was now on a positive journey of love and revelation, and it was working. **I was TRUSTING GOD.**

It took a few months to work on me. On **April 24, 2016, I met Jully Black**. She spoke at an event that I wasn't even supposed to be at, but I ended up there to support a friend who was on the panel of speakers. Jully's testimony spoke to me, and I was in tears. I couldn't stop bawling, so I went over to her and introduced myself. I expressed to her what her testimony did for me, and we literally bonded in seconds. She gave me her card and said to please message her. I told her I would, and I sent her the following message:

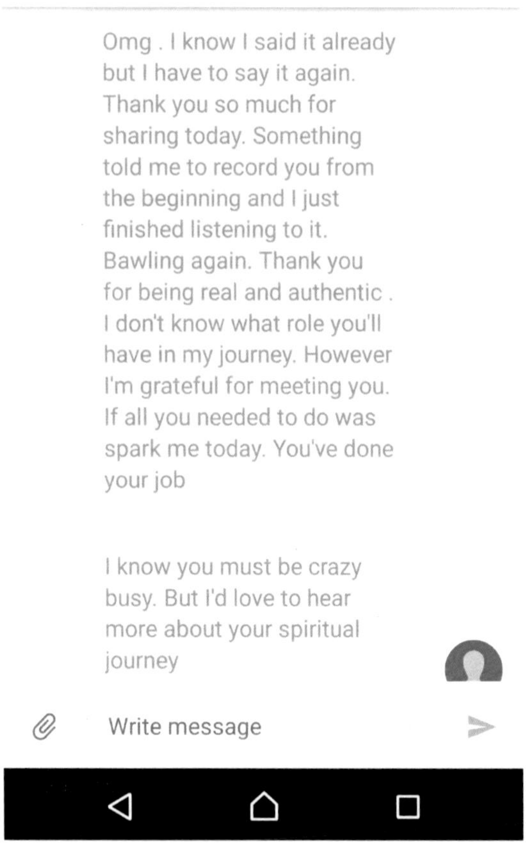

Omg . I know I said it already
but I have to say it again.
Thank you so much for
sharing today. Something
told me to record you from
the beginning and I just
finished listening to it.
Bawling again. Thank you
for being real and authentic .
I don't know what role you'll
have in my journey. However
I'm grateful for meeting you.
If all you needed to do was
spark me today. You've done
your job

I know you must be crazy
busy. But I'd love to hear
more about your spiritual
journey

Write message

We connected, and she added me to a private group of spiritual warriors. A group of people that were ready to be obedient and share GOD with the world. Attracting this group showed me that I knew I wanted more out of all areas of my life, especially my love life. I wanted to really be loved, and I wanted to love someone because I felt like I have now taught myself how to love. I was falling in love with me, and I loved it. I was now able to look in the mirror and say, "Girl, I love me some you." I was on my way, and it felt great.

My journey is definitely not over. I actually feel as if it has just begun. In life, we go through stages, and the first will always connect to the next. We each have our own story and experiences, and I believe that they come along to help us grow into stronger human beings on this earth. I welcome the next stage of my life and what is to come. I know that God has an amazing plan, and He will forever guide my steps. He has brought me this far to fulfill His mission, and He will never leave me. ALWAYS REMEMBER THAT HE WILL DO THE SAME FOR YOU.

Each trial is meant to shape us and as long as we learn the lesson that was intended, we will always overcome adversity. I have now conquered my issue of low self-esteem and body image, and I am learning everyday to live in love and by faith to overcome depression. I desire to progress completely into the next stage which is OPENNESS. I have recognized that my future is bright and that I do have a purpose to fulfill. That purpose does not include the past, so I am not looking back. I am planning for the future. **THERE IS A LIFE AFTER DIVORCE, EVEN IF THAT INCLUDES ONLINE DATING. I developed a new PHD ~ Praising Him Daily.**

Thank you for taking the time to read about my experiences and for choosing to get to know me. I am grateful to you for your choice and will cherish it forever. Don't ever underestimate the value of YOU and the power you possess. You are filled with the ability to be great because that is exactly how GOD created you. Listen to your GUT. It is GOD speaking. Know that all prayers are always answered and blessings are delivered on His terms. If you are asking, and you feel like you are not receiving, slow down, rethink and ask if you are on GOD's timing or yours.

Until you read again ~

Signed Your Sis,

Micca